STORY OF PROPHET ADAM (A.S)

SEEMA SUHANA

Contents

Contents

Contents

Foreword

These books gives us knowledge about our beloved Prophets in story form . Books are available on all e-sites such as Amazon (India , USA , UK) , Flipkart (India) , Snapdeal (India) , Booktopia (UK,USA) , Barneandnoble(UK,USA) Shopee (India) ,wordery (USA) ,Wob (UK), Libro (USA) , Notionpress . contact me on instagram @Soulful_suhana to order in bulk and to get great discounts on it

(A.S)-Alaihi Salam

These books are available in English , Hindi , Roman Urdu

English :

Book 1 : Story of Prophet Adam (A.S)

Book 2: Prophet Sheesh (A.S)

Book 3: Prophet Idrees (A.S)

Book 4 :Strom of Prophet Nuh (A.S)

Book 5 : Journey from heaven to strom (Story of Prophet Adam (A.S) from heaven to Prophet Nuh (A.S) in floods and strom)

Roman Urdu

Book 1 : " Kahani Adam (A.S) Ki"

Book 2:"Hazrat Sheesh (A.S) "

Book 3: " Aknookh Yani Hazrat Idrees (A.S) "

Book 4 :"Toofan -e-Nuh "

(Story of Hazrat Nuh (A.S)"

Book 5 :"Arsh se Toofan Tak "

(Story of Hazrat Adam (A.S) in Jannah to Hazrat Nuh (A.S) In Floods And Strom)

Hindi

पुस्तक 1: पैगंबर आदम (अलैही सलाम) की कहानी

पुस्तक 2: पैगंबर शीश (अलैही सलाम)

पुस्तक 3: पैगंबर इदरीस (अलैही सलाम)

पुस्तक 4: पैगंबर नूह (अलैही सलाम) का तूफ़ान

पुस्तक 5: जन्नत से तूफ़ान तक

(पैगंबर आदम (अलैही सलाम) से पैगंबर नूह (अलैही सलाम) तक)

Acknowledgements

(A.S) Refers to Alaihi Salam

ALHAMDULLIAH FOR EVERYTHING

I also do Arabic calligraphy

Dm me to placed your customised order

Do follow me on

youtube channel: soulful suhana

instagram id : soulful_suhana

without prior permission of the author.

And also the book or any part of the book will be translated in any other language without permission of the author

CHAPTER I

World Before Prophet Adam (A.S)

Allah created the heavens and the earth in just 6 days and the Heaven was on the water.

The earth was completely empty, deserted, a dark layer was present over the sea. Only water was layered on the ground.

The first thing to be made was pen and everything that was in the world was written by the pen

Allah created the soil on the day of saturday , and on that day light was also separated from the darkness by Allah . Light was given name as Day and darkness was given the name as night

The light that remained in the sky in the night was given named as stars , moon . and the light that remained in the day was named as sun.

On Sunday, on earth , mountains were created and atmosphere was separated from water. The upper part of the water was declared as the sky and the lower part was declared as the sea.

On the day of Monday trees were created, every tree were create its own generation from its own seed.

on Tuesday Pain, Problems germs and bacteria were created.

On the day of wednesday Noor (charm) was created

On the day of Thursday, all the animals found in water and land were created.

And all the creations on the (Friday) between the last period of the day i.e. in between asar till night. Human was the last creation of Allah

Allah created human as the ruler of all the animals who are found on the earth and the water. Allah has created human into man and woman. *Allah provided food to human in form of trees , plants and animals.*

Allah wrote the creations of all creatures 50,000 years before the birth of the earth from the heaven and at that time his heaven was on water that means in starting heaven was on water.

Allah first created pen. Allah commanded pen to write . Pen wrote down everything that had happened until the Day of Resurrection. This is the knowledge of Allah , by which pen wrote everything. After the pen, everything was written on Preserved Tablet (loh-e -mehfooz)

Angels and Jinn were born before humans. First is angel, second jinn and last human.

Angels was created by light, Jinn by the flame of fire and human beings by fists.

The real place of angels is the sky. Angels are the one who are obedient of Allah

2000 years before Prophet Adam (A.S) , jinns were created , they were populated on our land i.e., on earth .Jinns created disturbance on earth . Allah sent Angels to fight with jinn . In this battle, angels destroyed jinns . angels forced jinns to take refuge in the sea

The angels killed all those jinns except Iblees as he was schlor and according to Allah 's command he was taken to Jannah and some of the jinns had to take refuge in the sea.

The Iblees performed one rak'ah in 7,000 years and 1,000-year to one shajda. Iblees asked Allah for his needs and said," O Allah , I wish to se lohe-mehfooz".

When Iblees went through loh-e-mehfooz , he went through one part in which it was written as " one servant of Allah who will worship Allah , and in the end will disbeliever because he does not perform a prostration. His worship shall not be accepted, and his name shall be named shaitan, and by Allah 's command he shall be brought out in disgrace and in a state of humiliation ."

Iblees wish to read more but at this point that angels gave pity on shaitan , the name which was written on loh-e mehfooz

Angel Jibrael , Angel Mikaeel , Angel Izrael all listened to Iblees , because of worshipness . Iblees was known as Sultan-Ul- Malaika which means " king of Paradise ."

CHAPTER II

Heaven Before Prophet Adam (A.S)

Why did Allah create our father (Prophet Adam (A.S)) ?., and created us to worship Allah .?

Allah is not in need of our worship. Rather, we need it Allah . Allah 's sky is beautiful and is the best. Allah is the owner of every thing .

He created the creation to show the signs of his names, such as signs of mercy, signs of nature, signs of power and signs of wisdom, otherwise Allah is not in need of anything.

Before creation of Prophet Adam (A.S) , Allah was asked about this from angels.

Allah says ""I have to place a successive authority (Khalifah) on the earth," , the khalifah means leader , and every one of his descendants will be the khalifah of the other , Who will establish government in the land prosper the earth and settled there

Allah created human from the fist of the earth and Allah only settled Prophet Adam (A.S) and his children in this earth. Allah 's intention was to populate human in the earth , prosper earth

Jinns did not deserve to populate , prosper the earth ,as they are not so wise that they could keep the earth beautiful and populated. The most intelligent of the jinn is who have the same capacity as a 10 year old child so the Ability to inhabit the earth was to human by Allah .

The Angels witnessed the vile acts and saw the unjust bloodshed in the earth as also the widespread corruption.

Allah created human with full of beauty then spirited soul .

Angels said to Allah " We consider You to be purified from every defect , Will You place one there who would create disorder and shed blood, while we intone Your litanies and sanctify Your name? , progeny of Jinn initiated bloodshed and envied each other and bore enmity with one another? "

and then Allah replied " Indeed I know what you don't know " (Sureh Al-Baqarah 2:30)

actually angels found out earlier that Prophet Adam's children will cause disorder and shed blood but angels did not talk about it as objection infact these kind of objection is sin and angels at any cost will not be disobiediant to Allah . angels will spend their entire life in praying Allah and live according to Allah 's order.

The statement the angels uttered was not a form of disputing neither with Allah 's decision, nor out of envy for the Children of Prophet Adam (A.S) or as some mistakenly thought. Allah has described Angels as those who do not precede Him in speaking, meaning that they do not ask Allah anything without His permission. When Allah informed them that He was going to create a creation on the earth and they had *knowledge, angel's only concern was that this creation (human) would commit mischief on earth.*

In this verse, Allah 's words "Indeed, I know that which you do not know" means, I know the benefit of creating this type of creature outweighs the harm that you mentioned, that which you have no knowledge of. I will create among them Prophets and send Messengers. I will also create among them truthful, martyrs, righteous believers, worshippers, the modest , the pious, the scholars who spread their knowledge to humble people and those who love Allah and follow His Messengers.

Therefore, angel's asking was question of amaze, only asking for reason for man's creation as angels had seen the deeds of jinn on earth.

When Allah created Jinn and gave them all the powers , instead of creating peace on earth, prosper earth they rather destroyed it

Angels were thinking Allah decided to create a new creation who will fight with each other , will they follow jinns inimitable step, so angels question to Allah was not Allah 's disobedience but the question on the face of surprise like will human be also like jinns

On the other hand angels also thought that they had failed in the worship of Allah , which led to the new creation by Allah .

There was another thing in angel's mind on this matter they said to each other that whatever Allah creates will not be more learned than us, we have special place , we will never disbelieve in Allah , we angels enforces Allah 's command in the heavens and the earth.

CHAPTER III

The Creation Of Humans In Four Ways

Allah created human in four ways

1. Without men, and woman Allah created man with a fist, and he is The Prophet Adam.

2 . Hawwa (A.S) was created from the left rib of Prophet Adam (A.S).

3 . From combination of both men and women ordinary human beings are born.

4 . woman alone create a man who is Essa (A.S) who was created from Holy woman Maryam (A.S) without father.

This incident leads to a few reasons

Allah is not bounded to create human beings in the same way, but he is such a great power that he can create man in any way he wants.

It was possible that Men would think that if we would not have been there, no human being was created.

It was also possible that woman would think that if we would not have been there, no human being was created.

Similarly, both men and women would assume that we men and women do not exist, which no human being was born

CHAPTER IV

Birth Of Prophet Adam (A.S)

By Allah's command, the earth came into existence, and the earth became the best place to live.

When Allah created Prophet Adam (A.S) , He commanded Angel to bring the soil of the earth.

When Allah sent Angel Jibrael to bring a handful of fist from the earth for the creation of Adam (A.S) , then Angel Jibrael went on earth as per Allah's command, the earth said, "I seek refuge of Allah from you taking away my soil."

Earth said " I give you to swere of Allah , I dont want my fist to get involve in such creation who will commit sin and will receive punishment from Allah . I dont have ability to take punishment from Allah . "

Angel Jibrael returned and said to Allah , " O Allah you know better the earth has sworn by you. "

Then Angel Mikaeel went to collect fist, the earth sent him empty hand too , again prayed for Allah 's refuge .

Then Angel Israfeal went to collect fist , the earth sent him empty hand too , again prayed for Allah 's refuge .

Then Allah commanded Angel Izrael (the angel of death) to bring a fist from the earth, Angel Izrael came to the earth, the earth again gave swore to him of Allah .

on this Angel Izrael said " you are giving me swore of him , who created me and you and is knowledgeable of everything for this work I am appointed by Allah , for Allah .Angel Izarel raised his hand and picked up fist and returned to Jannah ."

Angel Izrael said, "O Allah , you know everything, I have brought a fist. I have not accepted the oath that the earth gave me.

Allah said, Now you have been imposed on the earth, and from this fist I will create Prophets and I impose you on them

When I order you will take their soul.

Angel Izrael said, "O Allah , your servants will make me their enemy"

And Allah said, "you do not care about it, I will smitten them in one or other thing so that no one will consider you to be their enemy, eating more food will be cause of their death, some of them will be martyred , some will be die due to illness and no one will have any enmity with you , their will be some or the other reason behind their death

And the fist was brought to Allah . This fist was taken from the whole earth by Allah .

A part of this fist was taken from Mecca where there is kaaba today . Sand near kaaba was in the some mountain formthats why some part of the sand would touch water where water comes to a standstill.

Dry sand was used for existence of Prophet Adam (A.S) . That is why the children of Prophet Adam (A.S) appeared in terms of the earth, some are of white colour, some are black and some are in the middle of it, i.e., brown

Man's creation started with clay.

This sand is mixed with water because of which the word "tourab" has appeared in the Qur'an, tourab refers mixture of sand with water.

When this soil , fist was sown into water, it began to turn into clay , then Allah made a statue of man with that clay.

Allah first moulded man in the form of a statue and then left this statue for a particular period of time this wet soil dried up and colour became black , even it started to smell then it turned out into dry clay and finally the dry clay was cooked on fire

It was in the form of a perfect earthen vessel which is made of clay.

This was done on the day of friday . The days of us and Allah are different. Prophet Adam (A.S) remained in that form for 40 night , the body was present but there was no soul.

Prophet Adam (A.S) was created directly by the hands of Allah from clay .

Allah created Prophet Adam (A.S) and Prophet Adam (A.S) was very tall. As it is the evident from following Hadith: Narrated by Abu Huraira: The Prophet (S.A.W.) said, "Allah created Prophet Adam (A.S) , making him 60 ziras tall (about 40 meters) " (Al-Bukhari: 33:26) and since then the height of human being has been decreasing.

Before the spirit was passed into Prophet Adam (A.S) Once angels passed by him , angels were some what nervous by Prophet Adam (A.S) .

Among angels one jinn called Iblees was present among them. Iblees was a noble and elderly jinn . He did not disobey Allah like the other jins. So Iblees was at high place in Angel .

Allah rewarded the Iblees for his obedience, and Iblees was living in Jannah . Seeing Prophet Adam (A.S) , the Iblees had a little more nervousness . Iblees went around Prophet Adam (A.S) .

He saw that Prophet Adam (A.S) has stomach and understood that this creation would not control himself, by this we got to know that like humans, jinn and angel does not have a stomach.Only man is the one within whom the inside is hollow.

As the Iblees passed by, he would stumble upon the statue of The Prophet Adam (A.S) , and it would sound like empty hand on pot , and Iblees would say, "You are created for a particular purpose."

Saying this , Iblees would enter in the mouth of The Prophet Adam (A.S) and would go out of his waist and says to angels , "You have no need to be worry and get nervous."

If Prophet Adam (A.S) is imposed on me i will destroys Prophet Adam (A.S) , I will kill him and if he is imposed on me, so I will disobey him.

By this we know Iblees was astonished why Prophet Adam (A.S) was being created also by this we know how old is the enmity of the Iblees and Prophet Adam (A.S) .

The spirit was breathed into Prophet Adam (A.S) and Allah commanded , " When I breath my soul into it , you should prostrate before him . "

It is said that the Spirit refused to go into the dark statue , and Then Allah promised the Spirit that he would be withdrawn after a particular period of time

That is why the spirit goes to heaven after every human being dies.

When the spirit was breathed into Prophet Adam (A.S) , Prophet Adam (A.S) sneezed . Angels said say " Alhamdulillah " , Prophet Adam (A.S) agreed and he repeated the words said by angels

And then Allah said , " Rehamaka Rabuk " May your Lord have mercy on you.

When the spirit entered into the eyes and Prophet Adam (A.S) he saw the fruit of Jannah, on seeing those fruits brought worry to him.

When the spirit was in the stomach , Prophet Adam (A.S) felt the demand for food , now the spirit just entered till foot Prophet Adam (A.S) wished to eat .

When Allah created Prophet Adam (A.S) , Allah kept his hand on his back of Prophet Adam (A.S) so all the people who were born till the Day of Resurrection came into existence and presented it to Prophet Adam (A.S) within light of eyes of every human being.

Prophet Adam (A.S) asked, "Who are they o Allah ?"

Allah said " your children "

Allah questioned them "am I not your lord ?"

Everyone replied " yes you are our lord ."

All this was said by Allah because they could all become witnesses, and we would be punished for our sin and could not say we did not start shrik our ancestors did.

And Allah replied , I give you oppurtunity , that you should write down your destiny with knowledge that is in your hand , to commit sin or to virtue.

The glow of the forehead of one of the children of Prophet Adam (A.S) was attracted to Prophet Adam (A.S) .

Prophet Adam (A.S) asked Allah " who is he ?"

Allah said, This is a long way from your children his name is Dawood

Prophet Adam (A.S) asked " how old is his age ? "

Allah said , 60 years.

Prophet Adam (A.S) said include 40 years of age from mine into Dawood's age .

CHAPTER V

Disobedience Of Iblees

When Allah created Prophet Adam (A.S) and breathed his soul Allah ordered the angels (including Iblees) to prostrate in front of Prophet Adam (A.S) as a sign of respect

Angels prostrated Prophet Adam (A.S) by obeying Allah but, Iblees didn't as he thought he was better than Prophet Adam (A.S.).

The first prostration was prostrated Angel Jibrael

then Angel Mikael then by Angel Israfeel then Angel Izrael then the rest of Angels

Angel Jibrael was given the highest status i.e. the work of taking the commands of Allah to Prophets according to some scholars the first prostration of was performed by Angel Israfil so the Quran was written on his forehead.

Iblees was the only one who did not prostrate Prophet Adam (A.S)

Iblees was not one the angels who prostrated Prophet Adam (A.S)

Iblees thought, he is knowledgeable , after he worshipped Allah for many years and the same knowledge Prophet Adam (A.S) was getting instantly

Allah said to Iblees, " this command is for you also why did not prostrate Prophet Adam (A.S) are you considering yourself better than Adam , did I have not commanded all of you? "

Iblees did not answer, by saying "You have not commanded me, but , he gave reason for not prostrating Prophet Adam (A.S) , Iblees said " Why should I prostrate Adam, you created me from fire and made Adam from the fist , clay " iblees was proud of himself and jealous of Prophet Adam (A.S) Iblees thought he was better than Prophet Adam (A.S) . Iblees said, "I will not prostrate Prophet Adam (A.S) who is made of clay ."

on hearing words fron Iblees Allah commands Iblees , go out from here and you have no right to be arrogant in Jannah .

Because of Shaitan arrogance and disobedience to prostrate, Allah punishes him by expelling him from Jannah .

From then on, he has become shaitan from the Iblees.

Iblees asked Allah for respite , begged for the eternal life till the Day of Resurrection , Allah approved his petition and Shaitan was allowed eternal life until the Day of Resurrection. Shaitan was not grateful for the granting received by Allah towards him instead he threatened to mislead Prophet Adam (A.S) and his descendant from all directions to persuade them to leave the straight path, invite them to forbidden things, tempting them to abolish the religious orders and influence them not to be grateful to Allah for good deeds.

and when he got respite, he said to Prophet Adam (A.S) , " you mislead me and from here and after i will mislead you and your children ?"

Then Allah said to the cursed Iblees:

"Go with your followers who will be the fuel of hell. You will not be able to mislead My servants who have believed in me with all their heart and have a steady faith which will not be roared by your appeal."

Shaitan was removed from the ranks of angels and he became Prophet Adam (A.S) biggest enemy till the Day of Judgment.

The first sin is to be arrogant and the root of sins is arrogance

Iblees arrogance made the disbeliever. Disbelievers are the ones who deny the blessings of Allah

Iblees assurance that fire is better than soil was proven wrong the truth is soil is better *than fire*

soil nobleness that it is quite and serious since Prophet Adam (A.S) is made of soil on his sin ,Prophet Adam (A.S) repented , on driven out of Jannah, Prophet Adam (A.S) was taken into Jannah again

The glory of the fire is burning and destroying abilities

Iblees was damaged by his existence of fire.

He did not repent after sin, and was permanently condemned from Jannah

The nature of the fist is calm , Fire nature is of riots. fist arranged food for the man and animal. Their house and belongings are arranged by fist that is nothing similar to the fire.

fist is called prosperity, where as fire removes the prosperity.

CHAPTER VI

Prophet Adam (A.S) In Jannah

Allah commanded Angels to prostrate Prophet Adam (A.S) as Prophet Adam (A.S) was more knowledgeable,

This prostration is not a worshiper. Prostration was valid and permissible before , now it is haraam. Prostrating to Prophet Adam (A.S) by angels shows who is more capable and honourable.

Allah created Prophet Adam (A.S) with all knowledge of scholar. Allah created Prophet Adam (A.S) more knowledgeable than angels. Allah gave Prophet Adam (A.S) knowledge of the nature and reality of all things and everything .

When Allah sent soul to Prophet Adam (A.S) and Prophet Adam (A.S) stood on the foot

Allah commanded Prophet Adam (A.S) to go near angels and greet them by saying "assalamu alaikum "

language of Prophet Adam (A.S) and angels is Arabic and this language is off the heaven. angels replied to his greeting by saying Wa-Alaikum-Salaam

Allah said , " This is the how you and your children will greet with one another."

Allah taught The Prophet Adam (A.S) the name of everything like river , sea , tree anything that is present in world and Jannah

Allah taught the name of everything, like it's use , validity ,purpose

Allah has not given the Prophet Adam (A.S) a higher status only in the form of creation instead his status was higher in every form.

Allah said to angels, "Tell me the names of these things. If you are true in this

Allah commanded angels in this way because when Allah was creating Prophet Adam (A.S) angels said said Allah can create anything but he can't be more knowledgeable and schlor than us .

for this guarantee of them Allah commanded them " Inform Me of the names of these, if you are truthful." (Surah AL- Baqarah 2.31)

Then angels replied , " Glory to You (O Allah), we have no knowledge except what You have taught us. Indeed, it is You who is the All-Knowing, the All-Wise." (Surah AL-Baqrah 2.32)

Then Allah said to Prophet Adam (A.S) , " O Adam , inform them of their names. " .

Prophet Adam (A.S) informed the names of all things , Prophet Adam (A.S) did not do any mistake anywhere

Allah said, "Did I not tell you that I know the unknown of the heavens and the earth? And I know what you reveal and what you have concealed." (Surah AL- Baqarah 2.33)

Allah stated the virtue of Prophet Adam (A.S) above the angels, because He taught Prophet Adam, more than angels . Allah taught Prophet Adam (A.S) the names/ knowledge of everything, that is, the names of people , human, animal, sky, earth, land, sea, including the names of the other species. This occurred after Angels prostrated to Prophet Adam. This discussion proceeds only to show the importance of Prophet Adam's position, and the absence of the angel's knowledge about creating the Khalifah when they asked about it. This shows the Prophet Adam's superiority over Angels in knowledge.

As the years went by, Prophet Adam (A.S) lived alone for a long time in Jannah and it is in the Hadees that used to feel loneliness.

CHAPTER VII

The Birth of Hawwa (A.S)

After that Allah created Hawwa (A.S) Allah did not create Hawwa (A.S) immediately after Prophet Adam (A.S)

by this we get to know the importance of a woman is in man's life.

A man has to wait for a particular period of time to bring wife into his life and to get support and love from his wife.

Finally, one day when Prophet Adam (A.S) was asleep Allah created Hawwa (A.S) from his left rib and made flesh grow in its place, while Prophet Adam (A.S) was asleep and unaware. Allah made Hawwa (A.S) a companion of Prophet Adam (A.S) . Hawwa (A.S) accompanied Prophet Adam (A.S) and became his life friend, eliminating his loneliness and completing his natural needs to develop offspring.

The existence of Hawwa (A.S) was created from Prophet Adam (A.S) himself . Hawwa (A.S) was not another creation of Allah but she was created from existence of Prophet Adam (A.S)

When Prophet Adam (A.S) woke up, he saw a woman sitting near him and he ask " who you are ? "

Hawwa (A.S) replied " women " .Then Prophet Adam (A.S) asked " why were you created ? " Hawwa (A.S) replied " to provide relieve and peace to you. "

When angels saw Prophet Adam (A.S) talking to a woman, they said, "Now another creation has been created ! "

And they said " Prophet Adam (A.S) knows the name of everything we should asked him about this women "

Angels asked " who the woman was ? " . Prophet Adam (A.S) replied " Hawwa (A.S) "

Angels asked Prophet Adam (A.S) " why her name is Hawwa (A.S) ? "

Prophet Adam (A.S) replied to them as Allah taught him everything

Prophet Adam (A.S) replied to Angels " her name is Hawwa (A.S) because she was born from living being ".

Prophet Adam (A.S) could answer Angels question as Allah taught and gave him knowledge of everything

woman was born from rib which is close to heart , thats why one should be kind and loving to woman

Hawwa (A.S) will be most beautiful women among all the women in the world

CHAPTER VIII

The Marriage Of Prophet Adam (A.S) And Hawwa (A.S)

The first relationship that Allah created in this universe was the relationship between Prophet Adam (A.S) and Hawwa (A.S) i.e. the relationship of husband and wife.

Every husband and wife will live together in Jannah.

Nikkah ceremony was held of Prophet Adam (A.S) and Hawwa (A.S) . Hawwa (A.S) was married to Prophet Adam (A.S)

Allah said " grant your wife her Meher"

Mehr is something that does not cost anyone's daughter, Meher i.e., the seal is a symbol, that this girl is the responsibility of the man she is married to until they are alive or till this marriage is continued

Man will earn bread and butter set rules for the family , woman will create a generation, she will train children ,will teach to follow rules.

Allah asked " Prophet Adam (A.S) to pay Meher i.e., the seal "

Prophet Adam (A.S) asked " how he can Meher i.e., seal was paid !"

Allah said to Prophet Adam (A.S) , " My beloved Mohammed will be in your generation , recite Durood send blessings to him this is only your Mehr"

CHAPTER IX

Prophet Adam (A.S) And Hawwa (A.S) In Jannah

Prophet Adam (A.S) and Hawwa (A.S) were living a happy life in Jannah .

Allah granted Prophet Adam (A.S) garment that hides the private parts of human which is beautiful in its own way .

It proves that Prophet Adam (A.S) was not naked in past.

Prophet Adam (A.S) didn't even know the knowledge of being naked, nor his wife was aware of being unscreened.

Allah said to Prophet Adam (A.S) " O Adam, both you and your spouse live in the Jannah , eat freely to your fill wherever you like, visit anywhere in Jannah whose lenghth and breath is unimagable except for the fruit of the forbidden tree , or you will become transgressors/wrongdoers." (surah - Al-

Baqarah 2:35)

Allah 's statement was basically a test for Prophet Adam (A.S) and Hawwa (A.S) .

Allah has already warned Prophet Adam (A.S) When the shaitan was expelled from Jannah . Allah said to Prophet Adam (A.S) , " O Adam (A.S) , he is the enemy of you and your wife ."

There are different opinions over the nature of the tree mentioned here. Some said that it was the grape tree, barley, date tree, fig tree and so forth (neither Allah has mentioned anything in the Quran nor there is any authentic Hadith about the nature of this tree). The point here is that Allah forbade Prophet Adam (A.S) and his wife from eating from a certain tree in Paradise.

Prophet Adam (A.S) and Hawwa (A.S) understood that they were forbidden to eat the fruit of that tree.

CHAPTER X

Iblees i.e., Shaitan's Plan To Take Revenge

Shaitan was been expelled from Jannah.

Seeing Prophet Adam (A.S) and Hawwa (A.S) in Jannah, Shaitan was jealous of them Because he thought that all his disgrace was because of Prophet Adam (A.S) because he refused to prostrate himself to Prophet Adam (A.S) .

Hence he declared Prophet Adam (A.S) as his enemy and always wanted to take revenge and thus he would do planing and plotting to take his revenge

Because of shaintan's expulsion from Jannah, shaitan had enemity for Prophet Adam (A.S) in his heart.

when it was found to him that Prophet Adam (A.S) and Hawwa (A.S) were allowed to eat all the fruit of Jannah, but wheat grain is forbidden from eating.

So he left from earth to enter into Jannah.

Shaitan's entry was forbidden in Jannah, but he remembers three of those recitations because of their power of recitation that he could reach to the gates of Jannah.

He sat at the gates of Jannah. and waited for 300 years for someone to come out of Jannah and he could speak to him of words of his means.

CHAPTER XI

Help Of Snake And Peacock to Shaitan

Snake and Peacock also lived in Jannah.

they oftenly used to come and go in Jannah

one day Peacock and Snake came out of Jannah

When snake used to live in Jannah his mouth smelled with fragrances , also he even had feet although he dont have it today

and peacock was even beautiful than today is ., although today his feet was also beautiful

When Shaitan said to peacock and Snake to take him to Jannah, they replied, We fear Allah and we cannot take you inside of Jannah on peacock and snake's reply Shaitan gave them promises of their friendship that we have all been together in Jannah, take me in Jannah too.

If you take me inside Jannah , I will tell you three things in which you will have a never ending life.

You will not even have any disease and illness, and you will always be in Jannah.

Snake said to shaitan , do one thing you become snake and peacock will swallow you up, and go to Jannah and vomit you in Jannah.

Shaitan instantly became snake and peacock swallowed him And went to Jannah and vomitted shaitan in Jannah

Allah took away the beauty of Peacock to bring Shaitan to Jannah and also made peacock feet ugly as he brought shaitan with those feets .that is the reason why till today peacock feets are ugly and for snake with which mouth he advised peacock to help Shaitan, Allah took the fragrance of from his mouth and and filled with poisoned.

Allah said , "Allah will not have mercy on him who has mercy on you i.e., on snake " Therefore, killing snake is rewarded Peacock and Snake have been out of Jannah forever.

CHAPTER XII

Iblees Means Shaitan Again In Paradise

Shaitan went to Jannah with the help of Snake and peacock.

Peacock took Shaitan to Shaj-re-Mammua.

On the other hand, the guards of Jannah found that shaitan is in Jannah

When the guards came to take shaitan out of Jannah, Allah commanded let him remain stay may be Allah commanded because it was Prophet Adam (A.S) and Hawwa (A.S) 's test.

Now shaitan felt like to start his whispers and to take his revenge.

Both Prophet Adam (A.S) and Hawwa (A.S) were in Jannah by the command of Allah .

shaitan started trying to convince them.

Prophet Adam (A.S) and Hawwa (A.S) survived from eating fruit of the tree for a period of time, but shaitan, the enemy of the two, remained in trying and at the end through his strive he achieved what he wanted.

CHAPTER XIII

Shaitan Meeting With Hawwa (A.S) And The Prophet Adam (A.S)

Shaitan met Prophet Adam (A.S) and Hawwa (A.S) in Paradise and said , "I am your friend , why did'nt you both eaten the fruit of the tree yet " ?

He started to whisper "Shall I guide you to the tree of immortality and the eternal kingdom".

But Shaitan whispered to them to make apparent to them that which was concealed from them of their private parts.

Both of them couldn't recognize that cursed shaitan as his appearance had changed compared to the past.

Both of them said to shaitan, "Allah has asked us to stay away from that tree, and we have not yet eaten its fruit, yet and nor we will have this in future."

Shaitan said to Prophet Adam (A.S) , "I want you to always be happy in Paradise as you are living now ."

When Prophet Adam (A.S) heard Shaitan saying those words , he was deeply immersed in thought .

Shaitan said if you follow my words , you will surely have the power of paradise forever.

On hearing this, Prophet Adam (A.S) and Hawwa (A.S) came to Shaitan's and asked how it was a possible.

He said, "Your Lord did forbid you from this tree as Allah don't want you to become angels or become immortal." And he swore [by Allah] to them, "Indeed, I am to you from among the sincere advisors " (Surah Al -Aaraf 7:20 --21)

On hearing this, the heart of Prophet Adam (A.S) was filled with excitement , but he fear to disobey Allah came to his heart at another second

CHAPTER XIV

Shaitan Whispering To Prophet Adam (A.S) And Hawwa (A.S)

Shaitan was successful for creating confusion and doubt in the hearts of The Prophet Adam (A.S) and Hawwa (A.S) and shaitan fulfilled this in the form of giving greed in the hearts of both of them.

And the greed was, "This tree fruit is always eaten and will lead to an eternal kingdom and to become immortal "

the purpose of this whisper is to make their veiled body which is hidden from each other, exposed to both of them

Prophet Adam (A.S) and Hawwa (A.S) both were fully covered with clothes

Shaitan wanted Prophet Adam (A.S) and Hawwa (A.S) to disobey Allah .

Shaitan also gave them greed " Your Lord has forbidden both of you from this tree because you both do not become Angels and do not live forever " .

And shaitan swear in front of them, so that they will be convinced.

Shaitan also sweared by Allah , and from that time false statements , commitments , false oath were invented

CHAPTER XV

Shaitan's Plan Succeeded

Hawwa (A.S) came into shaitan's words. When The Prophet Adam (A.S) fell asleep , Shaitan came to Hawwa (A.S) and argued and convince her . shaitan testified snake.

Hawwa (A.S) came into Shaitan words and ate fruit.

The first of the two was Hawwa (A.S) who ate the fruit , she persuaded Prophet Adam (A.S) to make this mistake. Hawwa (A.S) and Prophet Adam (A.S) made a mistake.

When Prophet Adam (A.S) got up, Shaitan and Hawwa (A.S) convince And forced him and fed him fruit

Hawwa (A.S) said to Prophet Adam (A.S) " snake is the servant of Jannah and Shaitan is testifing snake . Now I am eating that fruit if anything happened then you should apologize to Allah , and if there is no need to apologize to all we will enjoy the pleasures "

Rasoolullah (peace and blessings of Allaah be upon him) said: "If Izrael had not been there, then the flesh would not been rotted and if Hawwa (A.S) , was not there Prophet Adam (A.S) would also not have been in a state of insolence. "

From this incident people have made thing that a woman is the reason of every evil, but it is not so , Allah forbade both of them to eat fruits.

CHAPTER XVI

Realization Of Prophet Adam (A.S) and Hawwa (A.S) of being undress

Iblees made them fall, through deception. And when they tasted of the tree, , their clothes fell their private parts became apparent to them, both Prophet Adam (A.S) and Hawwa (A.S) hided in bushes and they began to fasten together over themselves from the leaves of Paradise.

Both of them was shameful and embarrassed when they were undress, so it is in man's nature to not appreciated and accept to undress

It has come in the Hadith when Prophet Adam (A.S) was running away then Allah called upon and said " Adam are you running away from me "

Prophet Adam (A.S) said "I am ashamed of myself thats why i am running away also how can I stand before you undress as I had done this disobedience act "

Allah said to them, "Did I not forbid you from that tree and tell you that Satan is to you a clear enemy?" (surah Al- Aaraf 7:22)

CHAPTER XVII

Repentance Of Prophet Adam (A.S) And Hawwa (A.S)

Now, the point is, what priority did the two make on this matter?

Did they both stick to their own reasons which will bring them to arrogance , as if the Shaitan refused to prostrate , and then insisted on his own reasons and words .

did Prophet Adam (A.S) and Hawwa (A.S) repent?

Yes, both of them repented ,

both of them said, "O our Allah , Our Lord, we have wronged ourselves, and if You do not forgive us and have mercy upon us, we will surely be among the losers." (Surah Al -Aaraf)

CHAPTER XVIII

Prophet Adam (A.S) And Hawwa (A.S) Out From Paradise

Allah accepted their supplication and gave His forgiveness to them.

As mentioned in Quran:

Then Prophet Adam (A.S) received from his Lord [some] words, and Allah accepted his repentance. Indeed, it is Allah who is the Accepting of repentance, the Merciful. (Surah Al-Baqarah 2;37)

Both Prophet Adam (A.S) and Hawwa (A.S) left Jannah and descended upon the earth. Allah told them that the earth would be their realm and origin where they would live and die.

As mentioned in Quran:

Allah said, "Descend, being to one another enemies. And for you on the earth is a place of settlement and enjoyment for a time." He said, "Therein you will live, and therein you will die, and from it you will be brought forth." (Surah Al- Araf 7:24 --25)

Prophet Adam (A.S) descended on the earth and repented to his Lord.

Prophet Adam (A.S) was sent in India and Hawwa (A.S) was sent to Jeedah.

CHAPTER XIX

Increment Of Time For Prophet Adam (A.S) And Shaitan

when shaitan was asked to leave paradise and was sent to earth shaitan said , " O Allah , you brought me out of Jannah because of Prophet Adam (A.S) , and still I am coming out today , and I cannot dominate him without your help " .

Allah said , " I Impose you on him . "

He asked for more addition.

Allah said, "Whenever Prophet Adam (A.S) has children , you will have children here too."

He asked for more addition.

Allah said , " Their chests are your abode, you will be distant as the blood ."

When he asked for more addition,

Allah said, "Walk like horse , and players in chess game.your shaitan will share their wealth and children and be part of them."

The Prophet Adam (A.S) said, "O Allah , you have given Shaitan a long term increment and without your refuge I cannot be rescue from him , O Allah, You gave him power over my children and allowed him to control their mind and heart and penetrate every cell of their bodies. But what will you grant to my children ".

Allah said , " Whenever you have children here , I will grant one angel to protect them, angel who will protect him from shaitan . "

When Prophet Adam (A.S) asked for more addition, Allah said, " 10 good deeds will be rewarded for one good deed , and i will increase the reward in it too , and for one evil act only one sin will be added, and I will somehow erase it ."

When Prophet Adam (A.S) asked for more addition, Allah said , " As long as the children of Prophet Adam (A.S) are alive , I will not stop them from repenting . I will accept their repentance until their last breath. "

When Prophet Adam (A.S) asked for more, Allah said , " I will forgive their sins and will overlook their evil deeds. "

On this Prophet Adam (A.S) said to Allah " thats enough, "

{ So only Shaitan will be imposed on man, but the door to Allah 's guidance is very prosperous and easy, and man loses as he gets cheated by Shaitan's false promises}

CHAPTER XX

Events On Land

When downgraded to Earth, Prophet Adam (A.S) and Hawwa (A.S) were separated and was sent in two different places.

Prophet Adam (A.S) was sent down to India, while Hawwa (A.S) was sent to Jeddah.

When Prophet Adam (A.S) was sent from heaven to earth, he made his first step in Sarandeep i.e. Sri Lanka, the sign of which is found on the mountain of Sri Lanka.

Sri Lanka, which was earlier found to be a part of India, is now a free country. This mountain is also known as known as Adam's Peak and its height is 7,600 feet. It has a 5 feet 4 inch and 6 inch wide human foot mark.

Different religion has different stories with this foot mark we know Islam is the true one

With the blessings of Prophet Adam, there was blessing wealth and cultivation in India.

That is why India was first called the Bird of gold.

The shaitan was sent to the forest of Masaan, where the wall of Yajuj, Majuj is present today

and the snake was sent to Sajistan even today there is more snakes present there

It is said that if the tears of all human beings are collected, then there will not be as many as Hazrat Dawood (A.S) that fell on earth fearing from Allah

and then the tears of all human beings and Hazrat Dawood (A.S) are collected, then the tears of Prophet Adam (A.S) will be more than that

Prophet Adam (A.S) read this and prayed

"SubhanakAllah humma wabi humdika wata barakasmuka watala jadduka laa ee la ha anta zalamtu nafsi fagfirli innahu laa sagfiru Allah "

The repentance of Prophet Adam (A.S) was accepted on 10th Muharram.

Angel Jibrael (A.S) came to Prophet Adam (A.S) and brought 7 grains of wheat.

Prophet Adam (A.S) asked " what it is?"

Angel Jibrael (A.S) said " it is from the fruit of that tree as you were prevented from eating ".

Prophet Adam (A.S) said, "What can I do with it ?"

Angel Jibrael (A.S) said " sow the seeds in the ground "

Prophet Adam (A.S) sowed the seeds

The seeds of the Jannah were different from the worldly seeds , they were heavy and big in size

64

CHAPTER XXI

The Incident Of Bull And Prophet Adam (A.S)

After sowing grain in the land, Prophet Adam (A.S) brought bull to do irrigation

When bull was being lazy with Him, Prophet Adam (A.S) got angry with him and Prophet Adam (A.S) beat bull with a stick .Then bull said " if in the past if you would have not commited sin , today your position would have not been worse "

Prophet Adam (A.S) was sad after hearing this from bull and thereafter Allah command was passed and therefore, all the animals in the world today cannot speak.

Angel Jibrael (A.S) said, If you be strict with bull, it is not good of you , you keep being busy with your work.

When those grains grew Prophet Adam (A.S) harvested the crop , cleaned them , grinded them , kneded them , cooked them and thus after great hard work, he ate them.

CHAPTER XXII

The Re Union Of Prophet Adam (A.S) And Hawwa (A.S)

Prophet Adam (A.S) was extremely shameful of being sent to earth and also on the other hand Prophet Adam (A.S) was disturbed by being away from Hawwa (A.S)

Prophet Adam (A.S) spent many years of his life apologising to Allah

Ibn Asakar reported that Prophet Adam (A.S) wept for 60 years for his loss of Jannah and 70 years for his mistake. Allah accepted their repentance because it was sincere but also deprived them from the blessings of Jannah.

Allah showered mercy on The Prophet Adam (A.S) and one day Jibrael (A.S) came to Prophet Adam (A.S) and narrated forgiveness from Allah . Prophet Adam (A.S) was happy and thanked Allah .

Angel Jibrael (A.S) called upon Prophet Adam (A.S) to be thankful to Allah.

Prophet Adam (A.S) prostrated to thank Allah. Prophet Adam (A.S) went to mecca and built Kaaba exactly the same in saw in Jannah , Prophet Adam (A.S) also built Hajr-e-Aswad which is in the one corner side of kaaba , did tawaf like he saw angels doing in heaven

Prophet Adam (A.S) was the first to built kaaba . kaaba is built exactly below Baitul maboor

The Kaaba is the first house built by Prophet Adam (A.S) in the earth.

Angel Jibrael (A.S) said to Prophet Adam (A.S) that you are the first man and this kaaba is the first house built for the people.

The place where kaaba built was higher than the ground so the rain and flood water could not be found near it.

It is said that the place where Prophet Adam (A.S) prostrated is the place Kaaba is today.

The Qur'an mentions Mecca in the Qur'an, but mecca is also mentioned in as ummul kurra.

Um means mother and means kurra means place i.e. Mecca is the mother's place for all Muslims.

After tawaaf, Angel Jibrael (A.S) took him to Jible Arfaat.

Prophet Adam (A.S) and Hawwa (A.S) both searched for each other.

on Jible Arfaat , Hawwa (A.S) was present but due to separation many changes were occured in both of them.

Angel Jibrael (A.S) introduced both of them. It was here on Arafat that Prophet Adam (A.S) and Hawwa (A.S) were gathered and reunited like in Jannah. Allah then made Prophet Adam (A.S) the first Prophet on earth.

CHAPTER XXIII

Man In earth

Prophet Adam (A.S) knew that on earth, he had to face conflict and struggle. He had to protect himself, his wife and children from earthly creatures and hardships but above all, he had to struggle with the spirit of evil. The battle between good and evil is continuous but Prophet Adam (A.S) knew that those who follow Allah 's guidance and should fear nothing while those who disobey Allah and follow Shaitan will be damned along with him.

As mention in Quran:

And Allah said to them: "Go, all of you. When I send guidance, whoever follows it will neither have fear nor regret." (Surah-AL-Baqarah 2:38)

Prophet Adam (A.S), along with Hawwa (A.S) , started his life on earth. He knew that he was master of the earth and had to make it yield. He was the one who had to perpetuate, cultivate, construct and populate the earth.

He was also the one who had to procreate and raise children who would change and improve the earth. Time on Earth went on, Prophet Adam (A.S) grew steadily.

Allah began to spread mankind within the earth by men and women.

Then Prophet Adam (A.S) and Hawwa (A.S) witnessed the birth of their children, a set of twins

Hawwa (A.S) gave birth to 40 children by 20 times . Every time two children, a boy and a girl was born . Prophet Adam (A.S) and Hawwa (A.S) were blessed with many offspring.

The first twin was Kabeel and his sister Kameem.

The second twin was habeel and his sister labuda .

The growth and population started increasing.

Allah made The Prophet Adam (A.S) their Prophet . Prophet Adam (A.S) used to teach them religion of Islam.

Prophet Adam (A.S) is the Prophet and also the Messenger.

The difference between the Prophet and the Messenger is that the new Laws be revealed to the Messenger, and the Prophet is the master for the guidance of the people.

That is, every Messenger is a Prophet, but not every Prophet is a Messenger.

When Allah sent The Prophet Adam (A.S) to the earth, Prophet Adam (A.S) knew the art of work of everything.

kabeel And Habeel

The first sin in the earth came in the form of the murder of his brother Habeel at the hands of Kabeel.

Kabeel nature was ruthlessness , inhumanity arrogant, selfish and disobedient whereas his brother Habeel was intelligent, mercy , gentlemen ,obedient and always ready to the will of Allah as Allah blessed him with purity and compassion.

Kabeel was farmer and Habeel was Animal feeder

Habeel's soft heart is because of he was animal feeder

And in order to increase human population it was rule that is haram and invalid today , the rule was that man can marry his own sister except to the twin sister he was born with

In this case, Habeel's twin sister should be married to kabeel and kabeel's twin sister should be married to habeel

But sister of Habeel was less in beauty than Kabeel's sister. Therefore, Kabeel refused to marry Habeel's sister and wished to marry his twin sister, but to do this was haraam in the law of Prophet Adam (A.S).

" no one in Prophet Adam's law can marry his twin sister."

kabeel was very upset by law of Prophet Adam (A.S) .Kaabil became a rebel because of this law, he refused to accept Prophet Adam(A.S) law

CHAPTER XXV

Decision Between Two Sons

The Prophet Adam (A.S) decided between Habeel and Kabeel and ordered them to present a Hadiya before Allah .

Hadiya is the one animal who is to be slaughtered and distributed in the name of Allah .

The purpose is to present one's intentions for Allah . This process is called Qurbaani

In the time of Prophet Adam (A.S) , this sign of the sacrifice was that the fire would come from the sky and burned this sacrifice , which means that the sacrifice has been accepted and if the fire did not burnt, it means the sacrifice has not been accepted.

CHAPTER XXVI

Story Of Sacrifice Of Animal (Qurbani)

After all, the day of sacrifice came, Habeel took one of his best animals and brought it to the altar and presented it to Allah .

Kabeel, on the other hand, took one of his animals and offered it for sacrifice.

They saw that from the sky, a fire ball came and accepted habeel's animal on the other hand Kabeel's animal had not been touched by the fire.

Kabeel was very angry and said that Habeel's sacrifice was accepted because The Prophet Adam (A.S) had prayed for him and did not pray for me.

The Prophet Adam (A.S) said: "O Kabeel, your sister Kameem is forbidden to you, and halal on Habeel ."

Kabeel was very angry to hear this and tried to kill Kabeel, Habeel all the time.

Shaitan also Whispered to kabeel, "kill your brother" .

Shaitan came to the kabeel in human form and said, "The fire has eaten habeel's sacrifice, because he worships fire, so you worship too." Kabeel is the first person to worship fire so he is the first person to disobey Allah

CHAPTER XXVII

Intention To Kill Habeel

Kabeel decided to kill his brother. Until then, no man was been killed on the earth.

This is the first murder in human history, which Was chosen by Kabeel.

He went to his brother Habeel and said, " I will kill you " .

In response, Habeel said, "If you try to kill me, I will not raise my hand in my answer because ,I want you to take away my sin with your sin of my murder and therefore with your soul, my sins will be added to your sins and at the end your will be greater."

Training From Shaitan

Training from Shaitan

Kabeel did not understand how he can kill Habeel then Shaitan came to him in human form and snake was also with him.

Shaitan picked up the stone and killed snake and he died, so in this way Kabeel got trained by Shaitan

Habeel's Murder

One night Habeel was asleep , kabeel came to him with a stone of a dried layer.

Kabeel with anger and hatred hit the stone on his brother's head . He killed Habeel, he was one of the losers.

This is the first crime in the dark that took place by kabeel.

Habeel's testimony is the basic lesson

somewhere kabeel knew that after Prophet Adam (A.S) , the crown of prophecy will be adorned on Habeel's head, and this jealousy brought him down to the murder of his brother.

CHAPTER XXX

Allah Sent Crows

kabeel carried the brother's body on his waist and walked away.

Allah sent two crows They fought among themselves and One crow killed another one.

Now the living crow started digging the fists, took the dead crow, and put his fist on it.

In this way Kabeel found out how to bury. He buried the body of his brother Habeel.

Allah commanded the earth , " take habeel's blood within yourself " and the earth absorbed

CHAPTER XXXI

Kabeel Choosed Arrogance

Kabeel must be deeply ashamed of what he had done, but he did not apologize to Allah .

While it is neccessity for man if he commits sin he should, ask Forgiveness from Allah .

Kabeel was afraid of his father's anger.

On this occasion Shaitan gave Kabeel advice to run away from home, because if kabeel remains with The Prophet Adam (A.S), he would haved asked for forgiveness from Allah and would be on the right path after repentance.

Shaitan said to Kabeel, "Your father will not leave you , he will Kill you, then run away from here."

He fled to Yaman later he got married there he had many children.

In this way Kabeel lost contact with Prophet Adam (A.S) .

84

Allah has mentioned the story of kabeel and habeel in Surah -Al-Maaidah 5:27-31

CHAPTER XXXII

Starting Of Devoting Budh From Kabeel

Kabeel first started worshipping fire leaving all his father's religious authority behind.

and then Shaitan showed him method of making statue with a stone.

unlike Kabeel and his children left Allah and started the worshipping Budh a statue.

Prophet Sallallahu Alaihi wasallam Said "Whenever someone kills another person in world , a part of his sin will be added to first son of Prophet Adam (A.S) i.e.,kabeel because he is the first one who started the murder in the dark."

CHAPTER XXXIII

The Grave Of Habeel's

Prophet Adam (A.S) found out about Habeel and went in search of him but he could not find him

In this grief Prophet Adam (A.S) gave up eating and drinking.

Prophet Adam (A.S) was in grief as one of his sons is dead and other was won over by the Shaitan. At that time, Prophet Adam (A.S) started advising his children and grandchildren, telling them about Allah and calling them to believe in Him. Prophet Adam (A.S) told them about Shaitan and warned them by describing his own experience with Shaitan . Prophet Adam (A.S) also told them how Shaitan tempted kabeel to kill his own brother habeel . Further, Prophet Adam (A.S) also reminded them that humans have a real and eternal enemy that is a Shaitan. The shaitan will never stop and will never give up until the Day of Judgment to bring as many descendants of Prophet Adam (A.S) on the misleading path.

One day, when Prophet Adam (A.S) and Hawwa (A.S) saw Habeel in their dream,that Habeel was calling out to them,

due to uneasyness they got up from sleep and cried vigorously

At that time Angel Jibrael (A.S) came to them and narrated all things that happen with habeel and also what kabeel did to his brother.

Angel Jibrael (A.S) took Prophet Adam (A.S) and Hawwa (A.S) to habeel's grave . Prophet Adam (A.S) did'nt found any blood stains near habeels's grave .Angel Jibrael (A.S) said land had absorb up all your son's blood which was present at the time of habeel's murder .

The Prophet Adam (A.S) said, "Curse on the land of God, it soak the blood of my son, and then the earth swallowed up his blood .

Prophet Adam (A.S) and Hawwa (A.S) saw the their son with blood all over his body.

When Prophet Adam (A.S) saw this, he cried a lot, and kept habeel's body in a coffin and brought it to their place.

Whoever sees it was very sad, the birds would also say run away from man. he killed his own brother.

Prophet Adam (A.S) brought Habeel to his place and buried him.

CHAPTER XXXIV

Prophet Adam (A.S) And Hawwa (A.S) Were In Grief.

After the murder of Habeel, Hawwa (A.S) and Prophet Adam (A.S) used to be very sad, both of them were always in grief . Remembering Habeel, they used to weep all the time.

Prophet Adam (A.S) prayed to Allah : " O Allah , grant me child who is a believer of you and a help me in widening your religion in the world , and even after me he made sure your message is common in the world ".

CHAPTER XXXV

Birth Of Prophet Sheesh (A.S)

Both Prophet Adam (A.S) and Hawwa (A.S) were very sad about the murder of Habeel. they were always in grief and always prayed to Allah

Allah accepted the prayer of Prophet Adam (A.S) and Hawwa (A.S) and blessed him with a good noble son.

Prophet Adam (A.S) and Hawwa (A.S) were very happy with his birth.

Hawwa (A.S) named their beloved son Sheesh, which means "a beautiful gift from Allah ".

Prophet Sheesh (A.S) was much more beautiful and handsome than his father in terms of appearance and wisdom.

CHAPTER XXXVI

Upbringinng Of Prophet Sheesh (A.S)

Hawwa (A.S) and Prophet Adam (A.S) loved Prophet Sheesh (A.S) very much.

Prophet Adam (A.S) kept Prophet Sheesh (A.S) with him all the time .

They have come to know that this child will be their successor to the survivors of their childrens.

Prophet Adam (A.S) and Hawwa (A.S) concentrated in upbringing trained him in education from the very beginning.

Prophet Adam (A.S) used to refer to Jannah stories to Prophet Sheesh (A.S) and show him the difference of good and sack .

As Prophet Sheesh (A.S) grew older, his hidden education and parental training continued to take colour.

Prophet Adam (A.S) used to tell Prophet Sheesh (A.S) about the day and night and taught him about the prayer to be offered that was during these times.

He also informed about Storm of Noah and what came later.

Prophet Adam (A.S) and Hawwa (A.S) had expectations from Prophet Sheesh (A.S) because one of their sons had been killed and the other went in the guidance of Shaitan.

Now, in order to fight for the religion of Allah , fight with shaitan, after Prophet Adam (A.S) Prophet Sheesh (A.S) was the only one successor and hope

Prophet Sheesh (A.S) learnt different things from Prophet Adam (A.S), but he could not get all the knowledge of Prophet Adam (A.S), as he learnt from Allah.

CHAPTER XXXVII

The Real Story Worshiping Statues

There were some good people between Prophet Adam (A.S) and Prophet Sheesh (A.S) and others used to praise them for their good deeds and follow them.

Budha was a noble person, and he was a very beloved person of his people. When he died, his people his follower would sit surrounded by his grave and wipe tears

When shaitan saw them, he came as a man in human form and said, "I saw you crying, so what do you think ? , I can and want to make a picture of Budh for you?"

you keep this picture of him in your assembly and remember him when you see it in your assembly.

They agreed with the Shaitan So he made a picture of this noble man.

followers said, "If we keep his picture , we will have more passion in our prayers ."

And they used to keep the picture of Budh in their assembly and offer their prayers

And when they died and the second generation came, the shaitan explained them that their ancestors were worshipping picture.

When shaitaan saw this scene, of people sitting in the assembly worshipping the picture, he said to them , " should I keep a Budh's statue in every house of yours."

They agreed to shaitan's word and every one of them kept budh's statue in one's house thus budh's was mentioned in every house.

Then their children were said same thing by shaitan and practiced same then next generations came , they forgot that budh was a Noble man.

They brought him to worship as God, and then they began to worship this god, denying

Allah . Thus the first one to be prayed was the Budh a noble man who later was called God Budh .

95

CHAPTER XXXVIII

The Desire To Eat Jannah Fruit

When the time of the death of Prophet Adam (A.S) approached, he said to his children, "I heartly wish to eat the fruits of Paradise."

The fruits of paradise are and same like worldly fruits.

Apple , orange , pineapple etc all these fruits are present in paradise.

The difference between the fruits of paradise and the fruits of world is that the fruit of Jannah never gets rotten which is why they are never bad.

Similarly, fruits of the world are more temporary and the fruit of paradise are maintained.

Therefore, The Prophet Adam (A.S) wanted to eat the fruits of Paradise, and his sons went in search of Fruits

The Prophet Adam (A.S) said to his sons , "Go to Ka'bah and pray that Allah make my wish to eat fruit come true ."

after receiving order from father , Prophet Adam (A.S) son's took baskets and axe with them in search of fruits of paradise

They found Angel Jibrael(A.S) and other angels there, they had the shroud, fragrance, etc. of Prophet Adam (A.S).

Angel Jibrael (A.S) and other Angels, asked "What are Prophet Adam's children looking for ?" they replied and mentioned "Our father is a patient and ill and .his desire to eat fruit of Jannah.

Angels said, Come with us, we have brought with us the fruits of paradise.

Angels came in front of them in human form.

Angels said to Son's of Prophet Adam (A.S) , " Your father is nearing death ." nearly he dont have capacity to eat fruit

CHAPTER XXXIX

Prophet Adam (A.S) Commanded Prophet Sheesh (A.S) To Pray For Him

When Prophet Adam (A.S) fell ill, he wished to eat foods of Paradise he asked all his sons to get fruits of Paradise, a few sons went out in search of fruit towards forest, a few sons went out to Kaaba to pray that Allah grant them fruits of paradise so that their father's

wish could be fulfilled, but Prophet Sheesh (A.S) remained in the service of Prophet Adam (A.S).

When Prophet Adam's other sons who went to get fruit of Jannah and they failed to get fruits for him of Jannah

Then Prophet Adam (A.S) said to Prophet Sheesh (A.S) , " you go to Allah 's house kaaba and pray to Allah , and Allah will send me fruit with the blessings of your prayer " .

Prophet Sheesh (A.S) said: " you are my father , you are surely dear to him than me , you by praying Allah will surely send the fruit and your prayer will be accepted by Allah . "

On this Prophet Adam (A.S) said ," I am ashamed of the blessings of Allah for eating friut from tree in Jannah and you are clean ".

Prophet Sheesh (A.S) went there and prayed, and he saw That Angel Jibrael (A.S) was coming towards him with basket , and in this basket there was fruits and other dry fruits from Jannah, and another female angel hoor was appearing towards him by carrying basket on her head.

CHAPTER XL

Prophet Sheesh (A.S) Married To Hoor

When a Female Angel Hoor came with Angel Jibrael , Prophet Adam (A.S) asked Angel Jibrael (A.S) for whom this Female Angel Hoor was for.

Angel Jibrael (A.S) said: "Allah has sent this Hoor from heaven to Prophet Sheesh (A.S) because all your children were born by Allah in pair of a girl and a boy, except for Prophet Sheesh (A.S) so this Hoor has sent it to Prophet Sheesh (A.S)

After that Prophet Adam (A.S) accepted this Hoor and gave her to him in the provisions of Prophet Sheesh (A.S) .

The language of this Hoor was Arabic. The children of Prophet Sheesh (A.S) and Hoor also spoke Arabic

The Messenger of Allah Mohammed (peace and blessings of Allah be upon him) is also from the generation of Prophet Sheesh (A.S) and Hoor

CHAPTER XLI

Prophet Adam (A.S) Forgetting His Own Age

When Angels came to take the Soul of Prophet Adam (A.S) , he said say, "Forty (40) years are left in my age."

He was 960 years old at that time, and Prophets are well known of their age. Angels said, "Don't you remember that you have Given your child Prophet Dawood (A.S) forty (40) years of your age?"

by this we got to know that The Prophet Adam (A.S) refused, his children will Deny . Prophet Adam (A.S) himself forgot, his children were also forget things too. Prophet Adam (A.S) did sin , his children will also do sins

CHAPTER XLII

Advice From Prophet Adam (A.S)

At the time of Death of Prophet Adamapproached, he called his son Prophet Sheesh (A.S) near him.And he advised , " O my obedient son , you will be my successor . Do dhikr of Allah and whenever you mention Allah , do mention with him the name of his beloved Muhammad , I saw his name written on the Heaven at that time, when i was layered in the midst of the soul and the gritty

When I went round all the heavens, There he was, in all respects,

your glory in the Lord of Honour. I saw this word in which the name of Beloved Mohammed was there

when My Lord placed me in Paradise, I did not see a palace, any food, any window, any place where his name was not named, so you also mention them frequently.

CHAPTER XLIII

The Will Of Prophet Adam (A.S)

Prophet Adam (A.S) made Prophet Sheesh (A.S) as his caliph and successor at the time of his death and said his will to him that when strom of nuh strikes in the time of nuh and If you are at that time Then you keep my bones in ship. who will be saved from being destroyed or asked your children to do so in your will

Prophet Adam (A.S) wrote his blessings and will in a book in which was the message of Allah and Haidayath.

Prophet Adam (A.S) asked to protect book from Kabeel and his children as they couldn't damage book, nor they could change the book.

Prophet Adam (A.S) advised his son Prophet Sheesh (A.S) five (5) things in his will And he said, "You should also give this advice to your children, and that is my will and blessings."

- *Do not rely on the world and on its life Allah did not like my being satisfied with Paradise and finally I had to leave.*

- *And do not follow women's wish blindly . I followed the woman's wish and fed fruit from the tree and regreted it later*

- *Think about the end of what you want to do first, if I had thought about the end, it would have been easy not with Hoordles in life*

- *Don't do when your heart is not satisfied with doing because my heart was not satisfied and was shaking at the time of eating fruit .*

- *Consult in your work because if I had consulted, I would not have been in difficult situation in the same way.*

CHAPTER XLIV

The Death Of Prophet Adam (A.S)

Prophet Adam (A.S) made Prophet Sheesh (A.S) as his caliph and successor at the time of his death

Prophet Adam (A.S) the first human being and the first prophet, was also the first prophet to pass away from this world, after having lived for approx. thousand years.

Before his death, Prophet Adam (A.S) reassured his children that Allah would not leave man alone on earth but would sent His prophets to guide them. The prophets would have different names, traits and miracles but they would be united in one thing i-e the call to worship Allah alone. This was Prophet Adam's request to his children. Prophet Adam (A.S) finished speaking and closed his eyes. Then the Angels entered his room and surrounded him. When Prophet Adam (A.S) recognizes the Angle of Death among them, his heart smiled peacefully.

When the angels came to the take the soul of Prophet Adam (A.S) to be taken to Jannah . So Hawwa (A.S) recognized them.

She went near Prophet Adam (A.S) , cried aloud, and went to tight grip him.

The Prophet Adam (A.S) said, " get Separated from me. I had suffered because of you before, Get your hands on me and my Lord's Angels , then Angels took the soul of Prophet Adam (A.S), Gave them Ghusl, put on a shroud, smelled them , Dig the grave

Angels performed the funeral prayer of Prophet Adam (A.S) Then they brought Prophet Adam (A.S) body down to the grave. Put a fist on top of them

Prophet Sheesh (A.S) followed the words and methods of Angel Jibrael (A.S) to Burial Prophet Adam (A.S)

And then Angels said, "O Prophet Adam's sons , this is the way for you to do so." Then the people were not known by the command of burial.

They don't know how kabeel buried his brother , So the Angles were sent to tell them how the burial ceremonies should perform

So it was thus known how to bury man by Angels

The only sin Prophet Adam (A.S) did was to eat the fall of the tree in the life of 960.

According to different narrations, the day Prophet Adam (A.S) died was Friday.

A year after the death of Prophet Adam (A.S) , Hawwa (A.S) also died and was buried near him .

CHAPTER XLV

Children Of Kabeel, Son of Prophet Adam (A.S)

There was some time loosen for the punishment of the kabeel, so that he may repent and be on the way.

He went to the far-flung and settled in The Fold.

Khanook was born to kabeel

Then

Indar was born to khanook

Then

Mahaveel was born to Indar

Then

Matusheel was born to Mahaveel

Then

Lamik was born to Matusheel

Then

Aamaal named a boy was born to Lamik , a boy in the house of deeds, the first man to collect good wealth.

Then

Shatubaal was born to Amaal here in the works of the first man who performed tabla and sarangi yajat.

Then

Toh-Bel-Tin was born in shatubaal's house. Toh-Bel-Tin Worked on tambi and iron

Then

Naumi named girl was born to Toh-Bel-Tin

Similarly, the disobedient children of Prophet Adam (A.S) continued.

CHAPTER XLVI

The statement Of the children of Prophet Adam (A.S)

Prophet Adam (A.S) saw 40,000 000 of his children and their children in his life.

Anush was born to Prophet Sheesh (A.S)

Prophet Sheesh (A.S) was 112 when Anush was born and Prophet Sheesh (A.S) lived 800 years and to Anush more boys and girls were born

kanan was born to Anush at that time Anush was 90 years old and after that Anush lived for 815 years. They were more birth of boys and girls.

When Kanan was 70 years old,in his house was born in Mehlael and after that Kanan lived for 40 years. They were more birth of boys and girls.

When Mehlael was was 65 years old, in their house Yarid was born, and after that, Mehlael lived for 830 years, and their was more birth of boys and girls.

When Yarid was 162, khanook was born , after which Yarid lived for 800 years. and after that, Mehlael lived for 830 years, and their was more birth of boys and girls.

When Khanook was 65 years old, in his house mattoshalak was born, after which Khanook lived for 800 years. They were more birth of boys and girls.

When Mattoshalak was 187 years old, in his house Lamic was born , after which Mattoshalak lived for 782 years. They were more birth of boys and girls.

When Lamic was 182, Prophet Noah (A.S) was born to him. He lived for nearly 1,000 years. They were more birth of boys and girls.

When Prophet Nuh (A.S) was 500, Sam Ham Yafiz was born to him.